Pickup Lines

The Ultimate Book of Pickup Lines. Over 200 Funny, Clever, Cheeky and Adult Pickup Lines and Comebacks

Puma Pants

www.southshorepublications.com

ISBN-13: 978-1517314361

ISBN-10: 1517314364

CONTENTS

Keep Out Of Reach Of Children!

This book does contain some naughty words and references to some pretty weird sexual stuff. It may also contain references to some certain areas of the human anatomy and refer to them with names that are also not suitable for kids. So don't let them get their grubby little mits on it and then hopefully we won't get sued! Thanks!

INRTODUCTION

So, you want to brush up on your pickup lines? Well at Puma Pants we have got your back. We know what it's like to approach a nice piece of crumpet, only to realize that you have nothing to say and to just end up standing there awkwardly looking at her chesticles.

We are also fully aware this this book is great for reading while you're honking out a dirt snake. So if it ends up being kept in the toilet, fair enough. We have come to terms with it. We have also made sure the pages are as non-absorbent as possible, so if you run out of toilet paper you couldn't use this book as a makeshift ass wipe even if you want to.

We have done our very best to ensure that the quality of the pickup lines in this book are as high as possible for guaranteed moistness every time. By using most of these pickup lines, women will instantly see you in their mind as some sort of majestic stallion, galloping in slow motion through the breaking waves on a golden shoreline, just as the sun peeks over the distant horizon and bathes you in its warming glow. However some women don't seem to be able to take a joke, so if you do get a slap round the chops, don't blame us.

Anyway, let's get on with making you into a complete studly dreamboat.

CHEEKY PICKUP LINES

I'm not staring at your boobs. I'm staring at your heart.

Did you sit in a pile of sugar? Cause you have a pretty sweet ass.

People call me *name*, but you can call me any time you like.

You know how they say skin is the largest organ on the human body? Not in my case.

I'm not trying to impress you or anything, but... I'm Batman.

Well, here I am. What were your other two wishes?

Wow! Are those real?

You're single. I'm single. Coincidence? I think not.

Roses are red, violets are blue, I suck at pickup lines... nice boobs.

What has 132 teeth and holds back the Incredible Hulk? My zipper.

With my IQ and your body, we could make a race of super children and conquer the earth!

[Sorry, I have a boyfriend] I have a math test tomorrow. [What?] Oh, I thought we were talking about things we could both cheat on!

Pick a number between one and ten. Wrong! You Lose. Take all your clothes off.

Do you want to see something swell?

Should I call you in the morning or nudge you?

I don't know you, but I think I love you already.

Smile if you want to sleep with me.

I'm a mind reader and yes I will sleep with you.

A-B-C-D-E-F-G R-U-D-T-F with me?

CLEVER PICKUP LINES

You see my friend over there? [Point to friend] He wants to know if YOU think I'm cute.

Do you know what my shirt is made of? Boyfriend material.

My buddies bet me that I wouldn't be able to start a conversation with the most beautiful girl in the bar. Wanna buy some drinks with their money?

You're the only girl I love right now, but in ten years, I'll love another girl. She'll call you 'Mommy.'

If I were to ask you out on a date, would your answer be the same as the answer to this question?

I bet you $20 you're gonna turn me down.

I'm not actually this tall. I'm just sitting on my wallet.

There's only one thing I want to change about you, and that's your last name.

Hello, I'm doing a survey. What line is more cheesy out of, 'Do you come here often?', 'What's your sign?', or 'Hello, I'm doing a survey'?

Do you have any raisins? [No] How about a date?

I have this magic watch and it's that you're not wearing any underwear, is that true? Oh wait, it's an hour fast.

Write the following on a napkin and give it to a cute girl: "Smile if you want to have sex with me." Watch her smile!

Hi, I have amnesia. Do I come here often?

CHEESY/SWEET PICKUP LINES

If you were a vegetable you'd be a cute-cumber.

If you were a fruit, you'd be a Fine-apple.

Excuse me, I think you have something in your eye. Oh wait, it's just a sparkle.

If I had a penny for every time I thought of you, I'd have exactly one cent, because you never leave my mind.

If I received a nickel for every time I saw someone as beautiful as you, I'd have five cents.

If nothing lasts forever, will you be my nothing?

Wouldn't we look cute on a wedding cake together?

What does it feel like to be the most beautiful girl in this room?

I wanna live in your socks so I can be with you every step of the way.

Are you accepting applications for your fan club?

WEIRD/RUDE PICKUP LINES

Roses are red, violets are blue, get in the van.

Your body is 65% water and I'm thirsty.

Did you read Dr. Seuss as a kid? Because green eggs and... damn!

If you were a booger I'd pick you.

My love for you is like a fart, I just can't hold it in.

Did you fart? Because you just blew me away.

I wish I was cross eyed, so I could see you twice.

You're so hot, that if you ate a piece of bread, you'd poop out toast!

Girl, if I were a fly, I'd be all over you, because you're the s**t!

You are so hot that I would marry your brother just to get into your family.

You're hotter than my deep fat fryer.

You're just like my little toe, because I'm going to bang you on every piece of furniture in my home.

I hope you like dragons, because I'll be dragon my balls across your face tonight.

Wanna go halves on a baby?

I'm hung like a tic tac. Wanna freshen your breath?

It's fine if you lost your virginity. I just want the box it came in.

Do you like whales? Cause we can go hump back at my place.

I last longer than a white crayon.

Excuse me, I am about to go masturbate and needed a name to go with the face.

Do you like tapes and CD's? Cause I'm gonna tape this d**k to your forehead so you can CD's nuts.

How do you like your eggs? Poached, scrambled or fertilized?

I'm so good that the NEIGHBORS will be having a cigarette when we're done.

On a scale from one to ten, how old are you?

I need to be married with a baby by next summer in order to get my 10 million dollar inheritance, what do you say?

Please tell your breasts to stop staring at my eyes.

I almost called heaven and for an angel, but then I met you...and I decided to just hope were a slut instead.

I only have one testicle. [Really?] Only one way to find out.

I wish I was toilet paper so I would touch your bum hole.

I put the "STD" in "STUD" now all I need is "U".

Do you want a drink? I can make a cherry pop and a banana cream at the same time.

RELIGIOUS/RACIAL PICKUP LINES

Are you from Ireland? Because my d**k's Dublin.

Are you from Africa? Kenya suck this d**k?

Are you African? Because you're a frican babe.

Do you have an Asian passport? Because I'm China get into your Japantees.

Are you Jewish? Because I'm beginning to think Jewish this d**k was in your mouth.

Are you Jewish? Cause you ISRAELI HOT.

You had me at Shalom.

Once you go Jew, nothing else will do.

Are you a Shiite? Because when I saw you, I said to myself, "She aiight".

Our parents engaged us when we were little... they must have forgotten to tell you.

Are you from India? Cause I'm trying to get In-di-a pants

Jamaican my d**k hard!

Would you allow me Dubai you a drink?

Are you from Iraq? Cause I like the way you Baghdad ass up.

You can also use some of these horrendous puns to make your own pickup lines:

Hungary (hungry)

Kenya (can ya)

Norway (no way)

Venice (when is)

Cayman (came in)

Tibet (to bed)

Bali (barely)

Irish (I wish)

CREEPY/DIRTY PICKUP LINES

Do you live in a corn field, cause I'm stalking you.

That's a nice dress. But it would look better in an evidence bag at my trial.

I'm fighting the urge to make you the happiest woman on earth tonight.

Hello are you married? [Yes] Well I didn't hear you say "happily".

Excuse me, but does this smell like chloroform to you?

What's the difference between jam and marmalade? I can't marmalade my d**k up your ass.

Are you going to kiss me or do I have to lie to my friends?

Can I buy you a drink or do you just want the money?

[Point at her butt] Pardon me, is this seat taken?

You're like pizza. Even when you are bad, you're good.

You're so hot I would pay to drink your dirty bath water.

My d**k just died. Would you mind if I buried it in your ass?

There will only be 7 planets left after I destroy Uranus.

You know what I like in a girl? My d**k.

You can call me cake, cause I'll go straight to your ass.

Are you hungry? Cause omelet you suck this d**k.

What's the difference between a Ferrari and an erection? I don't have a Ferrari.

[Look down at your crotch] Well? It's not just going to suck itself is it?

Hi, do you want to have my children? [No] OK, can we just practice then?

Do you come here often or do you want to wait until I get you home?

Do you know what winks and lasts for over an hour? [No] Wink.

Do you like Wendy's? Cause you're gonna love Wendy's nuts are slapping your chin!

Do you like long cocks on the beach?

Let's play Barbie. I'll be Ken and you can be the box I come in.

You remind me of my cousin. [How?] I want to f**k you so bad, but I know that I can't.

We should totally meet up for a pizza and f*8k. [No!] Pie and a f**k?

GEEKY PICKUP LINES

I know Jedi mind tricks. Go home with me tonight you will.

Honey, you've been looking for love in Alderaan places!

You're the Obi-wan for me.

Yoda one for me.

Once you make love to a man with Vulcan ears on you never go back.

Tell me of this thing you humans call (pause) love.

Earth woman, prepare to be probed!

Your mouth says, 'Shields up!', but your eyes say, 'A hull breach is imminent.'

I can't help it -- my eyes are trapped in the gravitational field of your breasts!

You make my software turn into hardware!

Are you sitting on the F5 key? Cause your ass is refreshing.

You can put a Trojan on my Hard Drive anytime.

You still use Internet Explorer? You must like it nice and slow.

You auto-complete me.

Are your pants a compressed file? Because I'd love to unzip them!

I googled your name earlier... I clicked on 'I'm Feeling Lucky.'

I wish you were Broadband, so I could get high-speed access.

Girl, you are hotter than the bottom of my laptop.

Are you a 90 degree angle? 'Cause you are looking right!

I can figure out the square root of any number in less than 10 seconds. What? You don't believe me? Well, then, let's try it with your phone number.

I'd sure like to take you back to my domain.

Are you a 45 degree angle? Because you're acute-y.

Could you replace my X without asking Y?

You're so hot, you denature my proteins.

Are you made of Copper and Tellurium? Because you are Cu-Te

Do you like Science? Because I've got my ion you!

I want to do you periodically on the table.

Do you want to extract some protein from my column?

Did it hurt? [Did what hurt?] I think you must have just fallen down from heaven, and re-entry would have caused some fairly serious heat issues for you.

How do you feel about group experiments?

I'm attracted to you like the Earth is attracted to the Sun - with a large force inversely proportional to the distance squared.

JOB SPECIFIC PICKUP LINES

Waitress

Do you like pudding? Cause I'll be pudding this d**k in your ass.

You just gave me a foot long.

You would be the perfect woman if your hair didn't smell like stale grease.

I can sweep you off of your practical waitress shoes.

Magician

Are you a magician? Because whenever I look at you, everyone else disappears.

Photographer

I'm not a photographer, but I can picture me and you together.

Are you a photographer? Because every time I look at you, I smile.

You flashed me first, I'm just returning the favor.

That's not the only Canon round here.

Is that a telephoto in your pants or are you just happy to see me?

Nurse

Do you have a Band-Aid? Because I just scraped my knee falling for you.

I was feeling a little off today, but you definitely turned me on.

I think I'm lacking some Vitamin U.

Well...you just cured my erectile dysfunction.

I've got a bone for you to examine.

Chef

Are you a chef? Because you've got some nice buns!

Want to lick my beater?

Hi, I want you to meat my balls.

Do you like dried fruit? Because you're raisin my d**k.

Librarian

I don't have a library card, but do you mind if I check you out?

Can you tell me where I can find a book about picking up hot librarians?

Artist

Did you paint you own ass? Because it's a work of art.

I find myself drawn to you.

Military

You have my privates standing at attention.

Wanna play war? I'll lay on the ground and you blow the f**k outta me!

Postal Worker

I could have sworn I saw you checking out my package.

Are you interested in taking care of my special overnight package?

Fancy making me your priority male?

Athlete

Do you run track? Cause I heard you Relay want this d**k.

PICKUP LINE COMEBACKS

Man: I'd really like to get into your pants.

Woman: No thanks. There's already one asshole in there.

Man: Haven't we met before?

Woman: Yes, I'm the receptionist at the STD Clinic.

Man: How do you like your eggs in the morning?

Woman: Unfertilized.

Man: If I could see you naked, I'd die happy.

Woman: If I saw you naked, I'd be happy to die too.

Man: What would you say if I asked you to marry me?

Woman: Nothing. I can't talk and laugh at the same time!

Man: Haven't I seen you someplace before?

Woman: Yes, that's why I don't go there anymore.

Man: Where have you been all my life?

Woman: Avoiding you.

Man: Is this seat taken?

Woman: No, and mine won't be either if you sit down.

Man: Hey, baby, what's your sign?

Woman: Do not enter.

Man: So what do you do for a living?

Woman: I'm a female impersonator.

Man: I would go till the end of the world just for you.

Woman: Would you stay there?

Older Man: Where have you been all my life?

Woman: For the first half of it, I probably wasn't born yet.

FINAL THOUGHTS

Well, that's it for this book! You are now an officially certified Puma Pants stud! Get out there and put your favorites to use on some unsuspecting skirt and watch your little black book fill up faster than a fat kid chasing an ice cream truck.

Thank you so much for taking a look at this book, we really appreciate it. If you would also consider taking the time to leave us an honest review on this book on Amazon I would be extremely appreciative of your feedback!

You can find links to all of books full of great humor of various types by simply searching for "Puma Pants" on Amazon. Thanks again for reading and I hopefully speak to you all in the next book!

Printed in Great Britain
by Amazon

76074173R00031